Dedication

To every childlike spirit, young or old, that has ever been lost, confused, talked about, or misunderstood. No matter what, it's not too late to get back to chasing your dreams.

IF I WERE BORN A
BUTTERFLY

Arneez Franklin

(in egg)
In this tree, there is only me,
But if you saw my
surroundings, you would
probably disagree.

In other words, it only feels like this because I really cannot see. Help! Can anyone hear me? Is anyone there? This feels like a nightmare.

I am lonely, and I think I am scared.

As another day in the dark passes me by, I close my eyes and imagine I can fly.

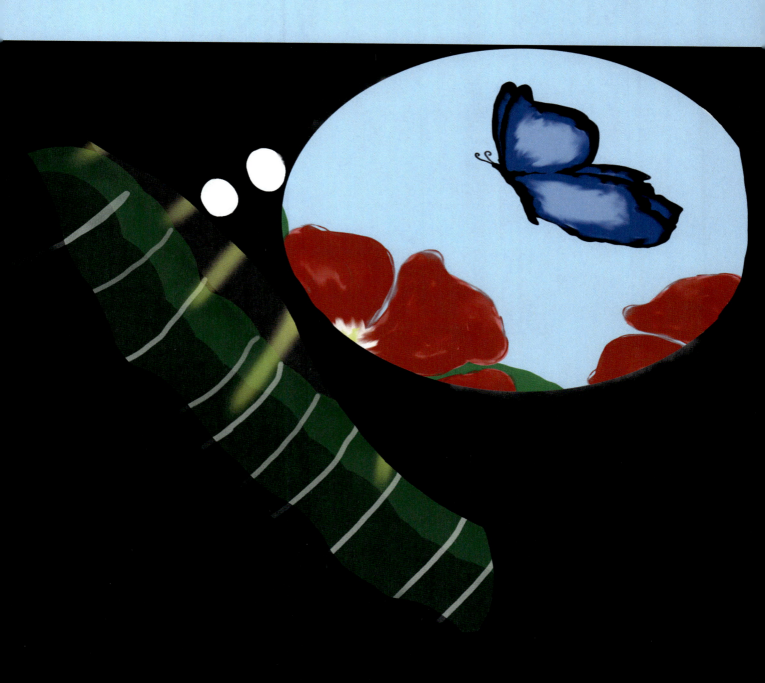

Good morning, great morning. To my surprise, I can see a crack of sunshine glimmering in my eyes.

As I puuuuuush and puuuuuuuuush my way through that wall, The things that were once set around me start to fall.

Down goes the shell of fear,
Down goes unfairness.
Down goes guilt,
And down goes being heartless
Down goes pride..
I can finally be
Who I really am inside.

I am FREE.
After that great escape.
I feel like a superhero,
though I have no cape.
It is time for me
To explore the world
and find my identity

[to a fly]
"Excuse me,"
"What?"
"Oh, sorry I bothered you,
But can I just have a
minute or two?
Who am I? "
"You look like a fat ugly green
caterpillar to me, goodbye!"

I feel a little heartbroken and cannot think of what to say. I feel tears in my eyes, so I just walk away.

I walk and cry until I fall over in exhaustion.
I then climb up into a nearby tree with caution.

[in cocoon]
In a world that is upside down,
I spin and I spin
around and around.
With my head faced
towards the ground,
I close my eyes and cover my
ears to block out all the sound

HELP! HELP! I am trapped once again. I am going to die this time for sure.

Why is this happening to me?
Why can't I just be happy?

Have I been captured
for dinner? If so, when
will all this be over?

I want to scream, and I have a lot of questions, But I do not want to act on my emotions.

Suddenly, I begin to move,
swaying from side to side.
Here it goes--I am sure
that now I will die.

Wooooosh,

Oh, it was just the wind
blowing, Moving the branches
on the tree, Swaying
from left to right
And right to left. You see?

Wooooosh, goes another gust of wind, Causing the tree branch to bend Down I go .

I have no control over anything, but I still hold onto hope.

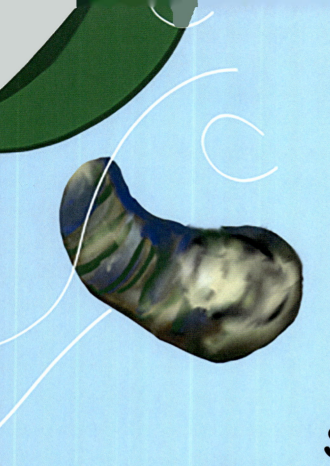

Splat!
I am free again.
The things that held me
back are now broken.

What is this feeling of
new healing? A sign of
new beginnings?
This is the feeling that
I have been seeking!

This time, I do not
have to force it.
The barriers have all split
with that one tumbling hit.

This time, I am not
looking down.

I am looking up.
Wait, look, I can fly......
Fly so high with my
head held high

Made in the USA
Monee, IL
26 June 2023